The Author's SOCIAL MEDIA Play Book

For Facebook

The Author's Social Media Playbook

The Author's Social Media Playbook For Facebook

Copyright © 2024
ISBN: 979-8-3211-9783-7

Printed in the Republic of Kenya
Published by:
Eword Publishers
P.O Box 70007, 00400, Nairobi
Tel: 0725 006 002 / 0745 420 420
Email: ewordpublishers@gmail.com

All rights reserved. This book or any portion thereof may not be reproduced or used in any manner whatsoever without the express written permission of the publisher except for the use of brief quotations in a fair book review or scholarly journal.

Table of Contents

Introduction
The Importance of Social Media for Authors 1
Why Choose Facebook? An Overview 3
Objectives of this Book 5

Understanding Facebook
History and Evolution of Facebook 7
The Anatomy of Facebook - Profiles, Pages, Groups, and More 10
Navigating the Facebook Interface 13

Building Your Author
Platform on Facebook 17
Setting Up an Author Page 17
Profile Optimization for Maximum Impact 20
The Role of Facebook Groups in Building a Community 23
Connecting with Other Authors and Industry Professionals 26

Content Strategies for Author
Defining Your Brand Voice 31
Content Mix - Balancing Promotional and Engaging Content 34

Creative Ideas for Content: Live Sessions, Q&A, Behind the Scenes, and More 36

Scheduling Content and Time Management 43

Facebook Advertising for Authors

Introduction to Facebook Ads Manager 47

Creating Your First Ad Campaign 50

Targeting the Right Audience 52

Budgeting and Bidding Strategies 55

Ad Auction and Bidding 56

Ad Formats and Creative Best Practices 57

Measuring Success: Understanding Key Metrics 60

Facebook Tools and Integrations

Using Facebook Pixel to Track Website Conversions 63

Integrating Facebook with Your Author Website and Other Social Media 65

Facebook Insights: Analyzing and Understanding Data 68

Leveraging Facebook for Book Launches and Promotions

Creating Buzz Before Your Book Launch 71

Running Promotions and Contests	74
Utilizing Facebook Events for Virtual and Physical Events	77
Collaborating with Book Bloggers and Influencers	80

Facebook Shops and E-commerce for Authors

Setting Up Facebook Shop	83
integration with E-Commerce	85
Selling Books and Merchandise Directly Through Facebook	86

Crisis Management and Online Etiquette

Handling Negative Feedback and Criticism	89
Managing Your Online Reputation	92
Staying Professional in the Digital Age	95

Staying Updated and Adapting to Changes

The Evolving Nature of Facebook and Social Media	99
Staying Informed on Industry Trends and Best Practices	102

Dedication

I dedicate this book to authors worldwide who strive to have their voices heard. Writing a book is a critical skill, but ensuring it reaches an audience is equally vital. I hope you will learn to utilize modern tools effectively, with Facebook being a key platform in this endeavor.

The Author's Social Media Playbook

Acknowledgement

I wish to express my sincere gratitude to God for making the publication of this book possible at this moment in time. For a long time, I have yearned to transform the inspirations He has placed in my heart into print, and now, it has come to fruition—blessed be His name. I also want to extend my heartfelt thanks to my wife, Esther Muthoni Karanja, for her support throughout my career. She has been a foundational pillar in all that I do. I am also grateful to Juniper and Mehitabel for being such lovely daughters and friends as I do this work.

I am immensely fortunate to work with a team that excels in the endeavor of writing and publishing. Their dedication is why I can expedite my work and maintain professionalism. I am particularly grateful to Hosanna Karanja, who has been the head of General operations and IT, for his research and editorial contribution to this book. My thanks go to Betty Karanja, our operations manager at Eword Publishers, for her supervisory role in getting this material ready. I am indebted to Mirriam Wangari for making this book accessible online to millions of readers worldwide. To the rest of the team, Priscilla Wangari, Bernice Wambui, and Stephen Ndung'u; your efforts in managing other aspects of our business have allowed us to concentrate on this project. Thank you all.

INTRODUCTION

The Importance of Social Media for Authors

As an author, understanding the importance of social media in today's digital age is crucial for building your brand, connecting with readers, and promoting your work effectively. Social media platforms offer unique opportunities to engage with your target audience, establish your online presence, and ultimately increase your book's visibility and sales. Among these platforms, Facebook stands out as a powerful tool that can greatly benefit authors in various ways.

Here are some key reasons why social media, including Facebook, is essential for authors:

- **Reach a Global Audience**: Social media platforms have billions of active users worldwide, making them an excellent channel to reach a vast and diverse audience. With Facebook's extensive user base, you can connect with readers from different demographics, cultures, and geographic locations. This global reach allows you to expand your fan base and gain exposure beyond your immediate network.

Introduction

- **Build Author-Reader Relationships:** Social media provides a direct and interactive channel for authors to engage with readers. It allows you to establish personal connections, build relationships, and foster a loyal community of fans. Through regular interactions, you can share insights, behind-the-scenes glimpses, and updates about your writing journey, fostering a sense of authenticity and accessibility that resonates with readers.
- **Promote Your Books and Events:** Social media platforms, including Facebook, provide authors with an effective means to promote their books, book launches, author events, and signings. You can create buzz around your upcoming releases, share book excerpts, reveal cover art, and announce book tour dates.
- **Establish Author Branding:** Social media allows authors to shape and showcase their unique brand identity. You can define your author persona, communicate your writing style, and differentiate yourself from other authors. Facebook provides tools to customize your author page, including profile information, cover images, and a consistent tone of voice, helping you create a recognizable and memorable brand presence.
- **Gain Valuable Insights:** Social media platforms offer valuable analytics and data insights that help authors understand their audience better. Facebook's built-in analytics tool, Facebook Insights, provides valuable metrics on post reach, engagement, and audience demographics.

Introduction

Why Choose Facebook? An Overview

Facebook has emerged as one of the leading social media platforms with its massive user base, diverse features, and extensive reach. In this section, we will explore the reasons why Facebook is an ideal platform for authors to connect with their audience and promote their work effectively.

- **Large User Base:** With over 2.8 billion monthly active users, Facebook offers unparalleled access to a vast audience. This user base encompasses individuals from various demographics, age groups, and interests, providing authors with a wide pool of potential readers to engage with.
- **Global Reach:** Facebook's reach extends across the globe, making it an excellent platform for authors seeking international exposure. Whether you are an established author or just starting your writing career.
- **Diverse Features:** Facebook offers a range of features that empower authors to showcase their work and interact with their audience in meaningful ways. From author pages and groups to events and live sessions, Facebook provides versatile tools to engage readers, share content, and foster a vibrant author community.
- **Visual Appeal:** Facebook's emphasis on visual content allows authors to showcase their books, covers, author events, and behind-the-scenes moments through compelling images and videos. Visual storytelling plays a vital role in capturing the attention of readers and igniting their interest in your work.

Introduction

- **Targeted Advertising:** Facebook's advertising capabilities enable authors to precisely target their desired audience based on demographics, interests, and behaviors. This level of targeting ensures that your book promotions and advertisements reach the most relevant audience, increasing the chances of engagement and conversions.
- **Viral Potential:** Facebook's sharing and engagement features make it conducive to the viral spread of content. If your posts resonate with readers and generate interest, they can quickly be shared, liked, and commented on, thereby increasing their visibility and potential reach.
- **Community Building:** Facebook offers a vibrant ecosystem of groups and communities, including those focused on literature, book clubs, and author fan groups. Authors can leverage these communities to connect with readers who share a passion for books, creating a sense of belonging and fostering meaningful discussions around their work.
- **Mobile Accessibility:** As a mobile-friendly platform, Facebook enables authors to engage with their audience on the go. Readers can access and interact with your content conveniently through their mobile devices, allowing for seamless engagement and connection.

By choosing Facebook as a primary social media platform, authors can tap into its extensive user base, diverse features, targeted advertising options, and viral potential to promote their books, engage readers, and build a strong author presence.

Introduction

Objectives of this Book

In this section, we will outline the objectives of this book, providing a glimpse into what you can expect to learn and achieve throughout your reading journey.

- **Comprehensive Guidance:** The primary objective of this book is to provide authors with comprehensive guidance on utilizing Facebook as a powerful marketing tool. You will gain a deep understanding of the platform's features, strategies, and best practices to effectively promote your books, engage with your audience, and build a successful author brand.
- **Practical Strategies:** You will learn how to optimize your author page, create engaging content, leverage Facebook advertising, and utilize various tools and integrations to enhance your social media presence. The strategies provided will be tailored specifically for authors.
- **Step-by-Step Instructions:** Throughout the book, we will provide step-by-step instructions, accompanied by screenshots and examples, to ensure clarity and ease of implementation. You will have a clear roadmap to follow, enabling you to navigate the Facebook platform effectively and execute successful marketing campaigns.
- **Case Studies:** To enhance your learning experience, we will include case studies of successful authors who have excelled at Facebook marketing. These case studies will showcase real-world examples, highlighting the strategies and tactics they employed to achieve remarkable results.

Introduction

- **Practical Tips and Resources:** In addition to strategies and case studies, we will offer practical tips, best practices, and resources to further support your social media marketing efforts. You will gain knowledge on topics such as crisis management, online etiquette, staying updated with industry changes, and managing your online reputation effectively.

- **Additional Resources:** To encourage continuous learning, the book will conclude with additional resources and references. These resources will include recommended books, blogs, websites, and tools that can assist you in further expanding your knowledge and staying informed about the ever-evolving world of social media marketing.

By the end of this book, our objective is for you to have a comprehensive understanding of Facebook as a marketing platform for authors and to feel confident in implementing effective social media strategies to achieve your marketing goals. We aim to empower you with the knowledge and tools necessary to build a thriving author platform, connect with your readers, and maximize the impact of your writing in the digital realm.

With the objectives set, let's dive into the subsequent chapters where we will explore Facebook's features, content strategies, advertising options, and more to help you establish a strong author presence on this influential social media platform.

Chapter 1

UNDERSTANDING FACEBOOK

History and Evolution of Facebook

In this section, we will explore the fascinating history and evolution of Facebook, tracing its journey from its inception to becoming one of the most influential social media platforms in the world.

The Birth of Facebook:

Facebook was founded by Mark Zuckerberg, along with his college roommates Eduardo Saverin, Andrew McCollum, Dustin Moskovitz, and Chris Hughes, in February 2004. Initially, the platform was created as a social networking site exclusively for Harvard University students, known as "TheFacebook."

Expansion to Other Universities:

After its launch at Harvard, Facebook quickly gained popularity among students. Mark Zuckerberg recognized its potential and expanded its availability to other Ivy League universities, and eventually to colleges and universities across the United States and Canada.

Understanding Facebook

Opening to the Public:
In 2006, Facebook made a significant move by opening its platform to the general public, allowing anyone with a valid email address to create an account. This decision fueled its user base growth and accelerated Facebook's position as a dominant player in the social media landscape.

Introduction of News Feed and Engagement Features:
In 2006, Facebook introduced the News Feed feature, which displayed a real-time stream of updates from users' friends and connections. This innovation transformed the way users consumed content and facilitated greater engagement on the platform. Features like the Like button, photo sharing, and commenting further enhanced the interactive nature of Facebook.

Acquisitions and Innovations:
Over the years, Facebook has made strategic acquisitions to expand its offerings and improve the user experience. Notable acquisitions include Instagram in 2012 and WhatsApp in 2014. These acquisitions helped Facebook diversify its services reach across different demographics and user preferences.

Mobile Revolution:
As smartphones became ubiquitous, Facebook recognized the shift in user behavior and invested heavily in mobile development. The introduction of Facebook's mobile app and mobile-optimized interfaces ensured that users could access and engage with the platform seamlessly on their mobile devices.

Understanding Facebook

Features and Enhancements:
Facebook continually evolves to meet the changing needs and preferences of its users. It has introduced numerous features and enhancements, including Facebook Live, Stories, Marketplace, Groups, Events, and Watch. These features have transformed Facebook into a multifaceted platform that caters to various interests and facilitates meaningful connections.

Social Impact and Influence:
Facebook's immense popularity and global reach have had significant social and cultural implications. It has revolutionized the way people communicate, share information, and connect with others. Facebook has played a pivotal role in shaping social movements, fostering communities, and providing a platform for expression and empowerment.

Understanding the history and evolution of Facebook is crucial for authors seeking to leverage the platform for marketing their books. It provides insights into its growth, features, and underlying principles that have made it a powerful tool for building communities, engaging audiences, and promoting content. In the following sections, we will delve deeper into the various components of Facebook, its interface, and the opportunities it offers for authors to establish their presence and connect with their readers.

Understanding Facebook

The Anatomy of Facebook - Profiles, Pages, Groups, and More

In this section, we will explore the different components that make up Facebook, including profiles, pages, groups, and additional features. Understanding the anatomy of Facebook will help authors navigate the platform effectively and make informed decisions about their social media marketing strategies.

Profiles:
Profiles are individual user accounts on Facebook. They represent personal identities and allow users to connect with friends, family, and acquaintances. As an author, you can create a personal profile to engage with your readers on a more personal level. However, it is important to note that using a personal profile solely for business purposes may violate Facebook's terms of service. Instead, we will focus on author pages for professional use.

Pages:
Facebook Pages are dedicated spaces for businesses, public figures, organizations, and, most importantly, authors. An author page allows you to establish your professional presence on Facebook and connect with your audience. Pages offer features tailored specifically for businesses, including insights, advertising options, and tools to engage with your followers effectively.

Understanding Facebook

Groups:
Facebook Groups are communities centered around shared interests, hobbies, or topics. As an author, you can create a Facebook Group to foster a community of readers who are passionate about your work. Groups provide a platform for discussions, exclusive content, and a closer interaction between you and your readers. It's an excellent way to build a loyal following and encourage meaningful conversations.

News Feed:
The News Feed is the central component of Facebook, where users can view updates, photos, videos, and other content shared by their friends, pages, and groups they follow. As an author, understanding how the News Feed algorithm works can help you optimize your content to reach a wider audience and increase engagement.

Facebook Live:
Facebook Live is a feature that allows users to broadcast live videos to their audience in real-time. As an author, you can use Facebook Live to conduct virtual author events, book readings, Q&A sessions, or behind-the-scenes glimpses into your writing process. It provides an interactive and immersive way to engage with your readers and build a deeper connection.

Understanding Facebook

Events:
Facebook Events enable you to create, promote, and manage events such as book launches, signings, webinars, or virtual author talks. Events can be shared with your followers and targeted audiences, allowing you to reach a wider audience and generate excitement and attendance for your events.

Messaging and Engagement:
Facebook offers various messaging and engagement features to facilitate direct communication with your audience. Messenger allows you to have private conversations, answer inquiries, and build relationships with your readers. Additionally, comments, likes, and shares on your posts provide opportunities for engagement and interaction.

Understanding the different components of Facebook will help you utilize the platform's features effectively as an author. By creating an author page, leveraging groups, and optimizing your content for the News Feed, you can establish a strong presence, connect with your readers, and promote your books in a meaningful and engaging manner. In the following chapters, we will delve deeper into each component, providing strategies and best practices to make the most out of these features.

Understanding FACEBOOK

Navigating the Facebook Interface

In this section, we will explore the Facebook interface and provide a guide on navigating the platform effectively. Understanding the different elements and functionalities will empower authors to make the most of their Facebook experience and optimize their social media marketing efforts.

News Feed and Home:
Upon logging into Facebook, you will be greeted by the News Feed, which displays a stream of updates, posts, and content from your friends, pages, and groups you follow. The Home button, usually located at the top left corner of the interface, allows you to return to the News Feed from any other page or section on Facebook.

Notifications:
Notifications are an essential part of the Facebook experience. They inform you about interactions on your posts, mentions, tags, group activities, and friend requests. The notifications icon, typically represented by a bell icon, is located at the top right corner of the interface. Clicking on it will display a dropdown menu with your recent notifications.

Navigation Menu:
The navigation menu, situated on the left side of the interface, provides quick access to various sections of Facebook. It includes links to your News Feed, Pages, Groups, Events, Marketplace, and more. You can also access specific features like Insights for your author page, Ads Manager for advertising campaigns, and Creator Studio for managing content and insights.

Understanding Facebook

Search:
The search bar, usually located at the top of the interface, enables you to search for people, pages, groups, events, and posts on Facebook. You can use it to discover relevant content, find new connections, or explore communities and topics of interest.

Author Page Dashboard:
As an author, your page dashboard is the central hub for managing your author page. It provides an overview of your page's performance, including page likes, post reach, engagement metrics, and more. The dashboard also allows you to create posts, access insights, manage settings, and interact with your audience.

Composer:
The composer is the tool you use to create and publish posts on your author page. It allows you to share text updates, photos, videos, links, and other multimedia content. The composer provides options to customize the audience for your posts, schedule posts for later, and boost posts through advertising.

Insights:
Insights provide valuable data and analytics about your author page's performance. They offer metrics on reach, engagement, likes, followers, and demographic information about your audience. Navigating to the Insights section of your author page will allow you to gain insights into your content's effectiveness and make informed decisions for your social media marketing strategy.

Understanding Facebook

Page Settings:

Page settings allow you to customize various aspects of your author page. You can manage page roles and permissions, adjust privacy settings, set up messaging preferences, and configure other options to align with your marketing goals and preferences.

Navigating the Facebook interface efficiently will streamline your social media marketing efforts as an author. By understanding the various sections, tools, and features, you can navigate the platform with ease, create compelling content, engage with your audience, and measure the impact of your efforts through insights. In the following chapters, we will delve deeper into specific strategies and techniques for building your author platform and optimizing your content on Facebook.

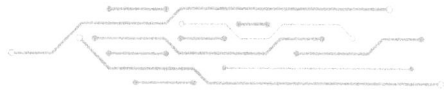

The Author's
SOCIAL MEDIA
Play Book

For Facebook

The Author's Social Media Playbook

Chapter 2
BUILDING YOUR AUTHOR PLATFORM ON FACEBOOK

Setting Up an Author Page

Setting Up an Author Page

In this section, we will guide you through the process of setting up an engaging and professional Facebook Author Page. Your author page will serve as the central hub for connecting with your readers, promoting your books, and building a loyal community of fans.

Create a Facebook Account (If You Don't Have One):
- To get started, you'll need a personal Facebook account. If you don't already have one, visit the Facebook website and sign up by providing your name, email address, date of birth, and creating a secure password. Having a personal account is necessary to manage your author page effectively.

Building Your Author Platform on Facebook

Choose the "Author" Category:
- Once you have a personal Facebook account, navigate to the "Create" dropdown menu located at the top right corner of the interface and select "Page." On the following page, choose the "Artist, Band, or Public Figure" category, and then select "Author" as the specific category for your page.

Enter Your Author Name and Category Details:
- In the "Page Name" field, enter your author name or pen name. Choose a name that is easily recognizable and consistent with your brand as an author. Add relevant category details, such as your genre, hometown, or any other information that helps readers identify your niche.

Upload a Profile Picture and Cover Photo:
- Select a professional and eye-catching profile picture that represents you as an author. This can be your author photo, your book cover, or your logo. Additionally, upload a compelling cover photo that showcases your latest book, your writing process, or an image that reflects your brand as an author.

Craft Your Page's About Section:
In the "About" section, provide a concise and engaging description of yourself as an author. Highlight your writing achievements, mention your genre, and share your passion for storytelling. Include links to your website, other social media profiles, and where readers can purchase your books.

Building Your Author Platform on Facebook

Set Up Page Vanity URL:
- Customize your page's URL (web address) to make it more user-friendly and memorable. In the page settings, look for the option to create a vanity URL using your author name or a variation of it. This will make it easier for readers to find and share your page.

Add Essential Page Tabs:
- Facebook allows you to customize the tabs on your author page. Ensure that the essential tabs, such as "Home," "About," "Posts," "Photos," and "Videos," are visible and easily accessible to visitors. These tabs provide a snapshot of your page's content and allow readers to explore your work further.

Adjust Page Settings and Privacy:
- Review and adjust your page settings to align with your marketing objectives and privacy preferences. You can manage posting preferences, message settings, and page visibility. Decide whether you want your page to be publicly visible or target specific geographic locations.

Invite Your Network to Like Your Page:
- Once your author page is set up, invite your friends, family, and existing readers to like and follow your page. Building an initial audience from your network will give your page a boost and create a foundation for organic growth.

Building Your Author Platform on Facebook

Profile Optimization for Maximum Impact

In this section, we will discuss the importance of optimizing your author page profile for maximum impact. By strategically enhancing your profile, you can attract more readers, establish credibility, and effectively communicate your brand as an author.

Update Your Profile Picture:
- Your profile picture is the visual representation of your author brand. Choose a high-quality image that reflects your professionalism and captures the essence of your writing. Consider using your author photo, a professionally designed logo, or an eye-catching image related to your genre.

- Example: Choose a professional author photo where you are well-presented and approachable. For instance, a clear headshot of you holding your latest book can showcase both your personality and your work.

Craft a Compelling Bio:
- Your profile bio is an opportunity to introduce yourself and engage readers. Write a concise and compelling bio that showcases your unique writing style, accomplishments, and the value you bring as an author. Highlight your notable publications, awards, or any other relevant information that sets you apart.

Building Your Author Platform on Facebook

- Example: "Bestselling author of heartwarming romance novels with a touch of mystery. I love creating stories that tug at your heartstrings. Winner of the Readers' Choice Award for 'A Love to Remember.' Get ready to embark on unforgettable journeys through the power of storytelling!"

Pin Important Posts:
- Facebook allows you to "pin" a post to the top of your page, ensuring it remains visible to visitors. Take advantage of this feature by pinning posts that highlight your latest release, an upcoming event, or any content that aligns with your marketing goals. Pinned posts grab attention and provide essential information to visitors.

- Example: Pin a post announcing your upcoming book launch event or virtual author talk. Include event details, dates, and how readers can participate. This pinned post will remain at the top of your page, ensuring visibility and engagement.

Utilize the Featured Photos Section:
- The featured photos section allows you to showcase a collection of images directly beneath your profile picture. Use this section to display your book covers, author event photos, reader testimonials, or any other visuals that provide a glimpse into your writing journey. Select high-quality, visually appealing images that resonate with your audience.

Building Your Author Platform on Facebook

Leverage the Call-to-Action Button:

- Facebook provides a customizable call-to-action (CTA) button on your author page. Take advantage of this feature by selecting an appropriate CTA that aligns with your objectives. Examples include "Learn More," "Shop Now," or "Contact Us." Directing readers to specific actions can drive engagement, book sales, or newsletter sign-ups.
- Example: Showcase your book covers as featured photos. Alternatively, display images of you engaging with readers during book signings or participating in literary festivals. High-quality and captivating images can pique readers' interest in your work.

Respond to Messages Promptly:

- Maintain a professional and responsive presence on Facebook by promptly responding to messages and inquiries from readers. Engaging with your audience in a timely manner demonstrates your dedication and fosters a positive connection with your readership.

- Example: Use the "Shop Now" CTA button to direct readers to your latest book available for purchase on your website or an online bookstore. Encourage them to explore your writing by providing easy access to your work.

Building Your Author Platform on Facebook

Optimizing your author page profile for maximum impact enhances your online presence and increases the chances of attracting and engaging readers. By crafting a compelling bio, incorporating relevant links, and utilizing key features like pinned posts and featured photos, you can effectively communicate your brand, build credibility, and capture the attention of your target audience. In the following sections, we will explore content strategies, engagement techniques, and advanced features to further strengthen your author platform on Facebook.

The Role of Facebook Groups in Building a Community

In this section, we will explore the significance of Facebook groups in building a thriving community of readers and fans. Facebook groups offer a more intimate and interactive space where you can connect with like-minded individuals, foster meaningful discussions, and cultivate a loyal following for your author brand.

Joining Relevant Facebook Groups:
- Identify and join existing Facebook groups that cater to your target audience, such as genre-specific reader groups, book clubs, or writing communities. These groups provide opportunities to engage with readers who are already interested in your genre or books. Actively participating in discussions within these groups allows you to establish yourself as an authority and build relationships with potential readers.

Building Your Author Platform on Facebook

Creating Your Own Facebook Group:
- Consider creating your own Facebook group dedicated to your author brand and readership. This gives you greater control over the group's direction and allows you to cultivate a community centered around your books. Make the group a place for readers to connect, share their thoughts, ask questions, and receive exclusive updates and content directly from you.

Setting Group Guidelines:
- Establish clear and concise group guidelines to ensure a positive and respectful environment. Specify the types of discussions allowed, encourage constructive criticism, and outline expectations for member behavior. By setting the tone early on, you can foster a supportive and engaging community that aligns with your brand values.

Encouraging Member Engagement:
- Actively engage with group members by posting regular updates, discussion prompts, and thought-provoking questions related to your books or writing process. Encourage members to share their thoughts, recommendations, and personal experiences. Respond promptly to comments, acknowledging and appreciating their contributions to the group.

Exclusive Content and Sneak Peeks:
- Reward group members with exclusive content, such as sneak peeks of upcoming books, behind-the-scenes insights into your writing process, or early access to cover reveals. Offering these perks creates a sense of belonging and makes members feel special, fostering their loyalty and enthusiasm for your work.

Hosting Virtual Events:
- Organize virtual events within your Facebook group, such as live Q&A sessions, author interviews, or virtual book clubs. These events provide opportunities for direct interaction with your readers, allowing you to deepen connections and generate buzz around your books.

Utilizing Group Announcements:
- Use the group announcements feature to make important announcements, share exciting news about your books, or promote upcoming events. Group announcements ensure that vital information reaches all members and helps create a sense of community by keeping everyone informed and involved.

Moderating and Nurturing the Community:
- As the group owner or moderator, actively moderate discussions, ensure adherence to the group guidelines, and address any issues or conflicts that may arise. Nurture the community by recognizing and appreciating members' contributions, and creating a positive atmosphere.

Building Your Author Platform on Facebook

Facebook groups provide an invaluable platform for building a passionate community of readers and fans. By joining relevant groups, creating your own group, fostering member engagement, and offering exclusive content, you can establish a vibrant and supportive community centered around your author brand. In the following sections, we will explore more strategies for connecting with other authors and industry professionals, as well as crafting compelling content to engage your Facebook audience.

Connecting with Other Authors and Industry Professionals

In this section, we will explore the importance of connecting with fellow authors and industry professionals on Facebook. Building relationships within the writing community can provide valuable support, and collaboration opportunities, and enhance your author platform.

Join Author Networking Groups:

- Search for and join Facebook groups specifically designed for authors. These groups serve as platforms for networking, sharing knowledge, and seeking advice. Engage in discussions, offer insights, and connect with authors who write in similar genres or share common interests. Building relationships with fellow authors can lead to potential collaborations, cross-promotion, and a supportive network.

Building Your Author Platform on Facebook

Attend Virtual Writing Events and Conferences:
- Many writing organizations and industry professionals host virtual events and conferences on Facebook. Join these events to connect with authors, editors, literary agents, and other professionals in the publishing industry. Participate in workshops, panels, and networking sessions to expand your knowledge, gain exposure, and establish valuable connections.

Engage with Author Pages and Posts:
- Interact with author pages that resonate with you or have a similar target audience. Like, comment, and share their posts to show support and foster engagement. Meaningful interactions with other authors can lead to reciprocal engagement, widening your reach and potentially introducing your work to their audience.

Collaborate on Cross-Promotions:
- Collaborate with other authors on Facebook by organizing cross-promotions, joint giveaways, or virtual author events. Partnering with authors who write in complementary genres can introduce your work to a new audience and vice versa. Explore opportunities for guest blogging, author interviews, or featuring each other's books on your respective platforms.

Create or Join Writing Challenges and Groups:
- Participate in writing challenges or create a dedicated Facebook group for writers to share their work, provide feedback, and engage in discussions.

- These platforms foster creativity, support, and camaraderie among authors. By actively participating and contributing to these communities, you can build connections, gain valuable insights, and find inspiration.

Attend Author Takeovers and Online Book Launches:
- Support fellow authors by attending their online book launches and author takeovers. Engage with their audience, ask questions, and show genuine interest in their work. This not only strengthens your relationship with the author but also expands your network as readers become familiar with your presence.

Share and Promote Other Authors' Work:
- Demonstrate your support for other authors by sharing and promoting their books, blog posts, or author events on your author page. This generous act of cross-promotion helps build goodwill within the writing community and encourages others to reciprocate.

Engage in Private Author Groups:
- Participate in private author groups where members discuss industry trends, marketing strategies, and publishing opportunities. These groups provide a more intimate space for in-depth conversations and collaboration. Actively contribute your expertise, seek advice, and engage with industry professionals who can offer valuable insights and guidance.

Building Your Author Platform on Facebook

- Connecting with other authors and industry professionals on Facebook can expand your network, provide support, and open doors to collaborative opportunities. By joining author networking groups, attending virtual writing events, engaging with author pages, and participating in cross-promotions, you can cultivate meaningful relationships and enhance your author platform. In the following chapters, we will delve into content strategies, Facebook advertising, and leveraging other features to amplify your author presence on Facebook.

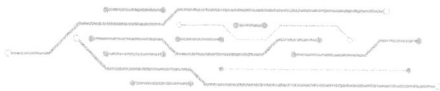

The Author's SOCIAL MEDIA Play Book

For Facebook

The Author's Social Media Playbook

Chapter 3

CONTENT STRATEGIES FOR AUTHORS

Defining Your Brand Voice

In this section, we will explore the importance of defining your brand voice and how it shapes your content strategy on Facebook. Your brand voice is the unique personality, tone, and style that sets you apart from other authors and helps you connect with your target audience.

Understand Your Target Audience:

- Before defining your brand voice, it's crucial to have a deep understanding of your target audience. Identify their demographics, interests, and preferences. Consider the genre you write in and the specific needs and desires of your readers. This knowledge will guide you in crafting a brand voice that resonates with your audience and effectively communicates your message.

Content Strategies for Authors

Define Your Author Persona:
- Think of your author persona as the fictional representation of yourself as an author. Consider the qualities, values, and characteristics you want to convey to your audience. Are you humorous, mysterious, or insightful? Are you an authority figure, a relatable friend, or a mentor? Clarify the attributes that align with your writing style and the impression you want to leave on readers.

Establish Consistency:
- Consistency is key to maintaining a strong brand voice. Ensure that your brand voice remains consistent across all your communication channels, including your author page, blog, website, and other social media platforms. This consistency builds trust, familiarity, and recognition among your audience.

Tone and Language:
- Determine the tone and language that best reflects your author persona and resonates with your audience. Consider the language choices, vocabulary, and sentence structure that align with your brand voice and appeal to your readers.

Inject Personality and Authenticity:
- Infuse your brand voice with personality and authenticity. Let your true self shine through your content. Avoid being overly generic or trying to mimic other authors. Authenticity attracts readers who connect with your genuine voice.

Showcase Your Expertise:
- If you have expertise or unique insights related to your writing genre, incorporate them into your brand voice. Position yourself as an expert in your field, sharing valuable information and perspectives that educate and engage your audience. This establishes credibility and enhances your author's brand.

Adaptability:
- While consistency is essential, your brand voice should also be adaptable to different types of content. Whether you're sharing book updates, behind-the-scenes moments, or writing advice, ensure your brand voice remains consistent while adapting to the context and purpose of each piece of content.

Emotional Connection:
- Strive to create an emotional connection with your readers through your brand voice. Emotions have a powerful impact on human decision-making, so evoke feelings that align with your writing and storytelling.

Defining your brand voice is a fundamental step in shaping your content strategy as an author on Facebook. By understanding your target audience, defining your author persona, maintaining consistency, injecting personality and authenticity, and adapting to different types of content, you can create a brand voice that resonates with readers and strengthens your author brand.

Content Strategies for Authors

Content Mix - Balancing Promotional and Engaging Content

In this section, we will discuss the importance of finding the right balance between promotional and engaging content on your Facebook author page. Developing a content mix that appeals to your audience and provides value will help you build a loyal following and drive engagement.

Understanding Promotional Content:
Promotional content refers to posts that directly promote your books, events, or other offerings. While it's essential to promote your work, striking the right balance is crucial. Too much promotional content can come across as pushy or sales-oriented, potentially turning off your audience. Aim for a balanced approach by interspersing promotional content with other engaging and valuable posts.

Providing Engaging and Valuable Content:
Engaging content focuses on capturing your audience's attention, sparking conversations, and encouraging interaction. It can include a variety of content types such as:

- Writing Tips and Advice: Share your writing expertise, offer tips, and answer common writing-related questions. This type of content provides value to aspiring writers in your audience and positions you as a knowledgeable authority.
- Behind-the-Scenes Insights: Take your audience behind the scenes of your writing process, research, or inspiration. Share snippets of your work-in-progress, character profiles, or excerpts to generate excitement and curiosity.

Content Strategies for Authors

- Book Recommendations: Recommend books you enjoyed reading within your genre or related genres. This not only provides value to your audience but also fosters a sense of community by connecting readers with other authors' works.

- Author Interviews: Conduct interviews with other authors or industry professionals. This allows you to provide valuable content while promoting fellow authors and building relationships within the writing community.

- Writing Challenges and Prompts: Engage your audience by sharing writing challenges or prompts. Encourage them to participate and share their work, fostering creativity and interaction.

- Fan Engagement: Create posts that specifically engage your fans and readers. Ask questions, conduct polls, and encourage them to share their thoughts, opinions, or experiences related to your books or writing.

Educate and Entertain:
While promoting your work is important, it's equally essential to entertain and educate your audience. Share interesting facts, writing-related trivia, or book-related news. Be creative and find ways to make your content informative, fun, and shareable.

Content Strategies for Authors

Visual Content:
Incorporate visual content such as images, graphics, and videos into your content mix. Visuals catch the eye, increase engagement, and help convey your message effectively. Use high-quality visuals that align with your brand and captivate your audience's attention.

Planning and Scheduling:
Develop a content calendar to plan and schedule your posts in advance. This allows you to maintain a consistent presence and ensures a balanced mix of promotional and engaging content. Use scheduling tools to streamline your posting process and save time.

Remember, the key to a successful content mix is finding the right balance between promotional and engaging content. By providing valuable, entertaining, and educational content, you can foster a loyal and engaged community of readers on your Facebook author page. In the next section, we will explore creative ideas for content, including live sessions, Q&A sessions, and storytelling through Facebook Stories.

Creative Ideas for Content: Live Sessions, Q&A, Behind the Scenes, and More

In this section, we will explore creative content ideas to engage your audience and enhance your Facebook presence as an author. By leveraging live sessions, Q&A sessions, behind-the-scenes glimpses, and more, you can connect with your readers on a deeper level and provide unique experiences.

Content Strategies for Authors

Live Sessions:
Live sessions on Facebook offer an excellent opportunity to engage with your audience in real-time. Consider hosting live Q&A sessions, author interviews, writing workshops, or book readings. This interactive format allows your audience to ask questions, share their thoughts, and feel a sense of connection with you as an author.

Q&A Sessions:
Dedicate a specific time to answer questions from your audience. Encourage them to submit questions in advance or ask them during the session. Q&A sessions provide valuable insights, address reader inquiries, and help establish a personal connection with your audience.

Behind-the-Scenes Glimpses:
Take your audience behind the scenes of your writing journey. Share insights into your research process, writing rituals, or the inspiration behind your stories. This behind-the-scenes content gives readers a glimpse into your creative process and adds a personal touch to your author brand.

Storytelling Through Facebook Stories:
Facebook Stories offer a temporary and immersive way to share content with your audience. Utilize this feature to share snippets of your writing, teasers for upcoming books, or exciting announcements. Engage your audience with captivating visual and textual elements.

Content Strategies for Authors

Book Recommendations and Reviews:
Share your favorite books within your genre or related genres. Write concise reviews or recommendations to spark discussions among your audience. This not only provides valuable content but also helps your readers discover new authors and expand their reading list.

Writing Tips and Advice:
Leverage your expertise as an author to provide writing tips and advice. Share practical insights, techniques, or exercises that can benefit aspiring writers. This content establishes you as a knowledgeable authority and strengthens your connection with fellow writers.

Author Spotlights:
Shine a spotlight on other authors in your genre or writing community. Interview them, feature their books, or collaborate on joint content. This not only provides valuable exposure for fellow authors but also introduces your audience to new voices and expands your network within the writing industry.

Fan Art and Fan Stories:
Encourage your audience to share their fan art or stories inspired by your books. Showcase their creativity and dedication by featuring their work on your page. This not only fosters a sense of community but also creates a platform for your readers to connect and engage with each other.

Host writing challenges or contests:
Your audience can participate and showcase their writing skills. Provide prompts, themes, or word limits to make it exciting and encourage participation. Recognize and appreciate the contributions of your audience by featuring the winning entries or offering small prizes.

Celebrate Milestones:
Acknowledge and celebrate significant milestones in your writing journey. Share the excitement of completing a manuscript, reaching a bestseller list, or receiving positive reviews. This allows your audience to share in your achievements and builds a sense of shared success.

By incorporating these creative content ideas into your Facebook marketing strategy, you can engage your audience, foster meaningful connections, and provide unique experiences. Remember to plan and schedule your content in advance, ensuring a consistent and engaging presence on your author page. In the next section, we will delve into storytelling through Facebook Stories and discuss effective content scheduling and time management.

Storytelling Through Facebook Stories

In this section, we will explore the power of storytelling through Facebook Stories. Facebook Stories provide a temporary and immersive way to engage your audience with visual and textual content. By utilizing this feature effectively, you can captivate your readers and create a unique storytelling experience.

Introduction to Facebook Stories:
Facebook Stories are short-lived, full-screen visual posts that disappear after 24 hours. They offer a creative and interactive way to share content with your audience. Stories can include images, videos, text overlays, stickers, and interactive elements, allowing you to craft engaging narratives.

Teasers for Upcoming Books:
Generate excitement and anticipation for your upcoming book releases by sharing teasers through Facebook Stories. Provide sneak peeks of cover designs, snippets of intriguing scenes, or quotes from the book. This teaser content builds curiosity and encourages your audience to stay connected and await the release.

Behind-the-Scenes Insights:
Take your audience behind the scenes of your writing process through Stories. Share glimpses of your writing space, research materials, or character development. Show the effort and dedication that goes into creating your stories, fostering a deeper connection with your readers.

Content Strategies for Authors

Author Events and Book Signings:
If you're attending author events or book signings, use Stories to document and share the experience in real-time. Capture the excitement, interactions with readers, and behind-the-scenes moments. This gives your audience a sense of participation and allows them to experience the event vicariously.

Interactive Polls and Questions:
Engage your audience through interactive elements in Stories. Utilize the polling feature to gather opinions, preferences, or feedback from your readers. Ask thought-provoking questions related to your books or writing process and encourage your audience to respond. This interaction creates a sense of involvement and encourages further engagement.

Exclusive Content:
Offer exclusive content to your audience through Stories. Share additional scenes, character sketches, or bonus material related to your books. Stories provide a sense of exclusivity as they are only available for a limited time, creating a special experience for your dedicated readers.

Story Highlights:
Utilize the Story Highlights feature to showcase your best Stories on your author page. Create highlights dedicated to specific books, events, or themes. This allows new visitors to catch up on important content they may have missed and provides a curated storytelling experience.

Content Strategies for Authors

Collaborations with Other Authors:
Collaborate with other authors through Stories. Create joint Stories featuring discussions, Q&A sessions, or special events. This cross-promotion introduces your audience to new authors and strengthens your network within the writing community.

Behind-the-Book Insights:
Share interesting anecdotes, inspirations, or challenges you encountered while writing a specific book. Offer insights into the story's origins, research process, or character inspirations. This behind-the-book content adds depth and intrigue to your storytelling.

Visual Storytelling:
Utilize the visual elements in Stories to enhance your storytelling. Use striking images, short videos, or captivating text overlays to create visually appealing narratives. Experiment with creative formats, such as sequential images that unfold a story or text overlays that reveal snippets of dialogue.

Storytelling through Facebook Stories offers a dynamic and interactive way to engage your audience with your writing journey and book releases. By incorporating teasers, behind-the-scenes insights, interactive polls, and exclusive content, you can captivate your readers and provide them with a unique storytelling experience. In the next section, we will discuss content scheduling and effective time management to optimize your Facebook marketing efforts.

Scheduling Content and Time Management

In this section, we will explore the importance of scheduling your content and effective time management for your Facebook marketing efforts. By implementing a content schedule and managing your time efficiently, you can maintain a consistent presence, engage your audience, and optimize your author platform on Facebook.

Content Calendar:
Develop a content calendar to plan and organize your Facebook posts in advance. This calendar should outline the type of content, posting frequency, and specific dates for each post. It helps you stay organized, ensures a consistent presence, and allows for strategic content distribution.

Strategic Timing:
Consider the optimal timing for your posts to reach the widest audience. Analyze your audience demographics and engagement patterns to determine the best times to post. Experiment with different posting times and use insights and analytics tools to evaluate the performance of your posts.

Automation and Scheduling Tools:
Utilize automation and scheduling tools to streamline your content posting process. Platforms like Facebook Creator Studio, Buffer, or Hootsuite allow you to schedule posts in advance, saving you time and effort. This enables you to maintain a consistent posting schedule even during busy periods.

Content Strategies for Authors

Batch Content Creation:
Maximize your productivity by batching your content creation. Set aside dedicated time to create multiple posts in one sitting. This approach allows you to focus on content creation without interruption and ensures a steady flow of content for your scheduled posts.

Mix of Evergreen and Timely Content:
Strive for a mix of evergreen and timely content in your posting schedule. Evergreen content remains relevant over time, such as writing tips, book recommendations, or behind-the-scenes insights. Timely content includes news or updates about your books, events, or current writing projects. This balance ensures a variety of content and keeps your audience engaged.

Repurposing Content:
Don't be afraid to repurpose your existing content to extend its reach. Turn a blog post into a Facebook post, transform a video into a short snippet for Stories, or create a quote graphic from a captivating line in your book. Repurposing content allows you to maximize its value and reach different segments of your audience.

Engagement and Response Time:
Allocate time each day to engage with your audience and respond to comments, messages, and inquiries. Promptly addressing your audience's interactions not only fosters a sense of connection but also helps build a loyal and engaged community.

Experimentation and Adaptation:
Continuously experiment with different content types, formats, and approaches to see what resonates best with your audience. Stay open to feedback and adapt your strategy based on audience preferences and evolving trends. This iterative process allows you to refine and optimize your content over time.

By implementing a content schedule, leveraging automation tools, and managing your time effectively, you can maintain a consistent presence on Facebook and optimize your content strategy. Balancing evergreen and timely content, repurposing existing content, and evaluating performance metrics ensure your efforts yield maximum impact. In the following chapters, we will explore Facebook advertising, utilizing Facebook tools, and leveraging the platform for book launches and promotions.

The Author's SOCIAL MEDIA *Play Book* For Facebook

The Author's Social Media Playbook

Chapter 4

FACEBOOK ADVERTISING FOR AUTHORS

Introduction to Facebook Ads Manager

In this chapter, we will explore how authors can leverage Facebook Ads Manager to create targeted and effective advertising campaigns. Facebook Ads Manager is a powerful tool that allows you to reach a broader audience, increase book sales, and promote your author brand. Let's dive into the basics of Facebook Ads Manager.

Understanding Facebook Ads Manager:
Facebook Ads Manager is a comprehensive platform that enables you to create, manage, and track your Facebook advertising campaigns. It provides you with tools to define your target audience, set budgets, design compelling ad creatives, and measure the performance of your campaigns.

Creating an Ads Manager Account:
To start using Facebook Ads Manager, you need to create an Ads Manager account. Visit the Facebook Ads Manager website and follow the steps to set up your account. Once your account is created, you can access the Ads Manager dashboard.

Facebook Advertising for Authors

Setting Advertising Objectives:

When creating an ad campaign, it's crucial to define your advertising objectives. Facebook Ads Manager offers various objectives to choose from, such as increasing brand awareness, driving website traffic, promoting book sales, or getting more engagement on your posts. Select the objective that aligns with your goals to optimize your campaign's performance.

Defining Target Audience:

One of the strengths of Facebook Ads Manager is its ability to target specific audiences. You can define your target audience based on demographics, interests, behaviors, and connections. For example, you can target readers who have shown an interest in your genre or those who follow related authors. Refining your audience ensures that your ads reach the right people who are more likely to engage with your content and convert into book sales.

Creating Compelling Ad Creatives:

Compelling ad creatives are crucial for capturing the attention of your target audience. Experiment with different ad formats, such as image ads, video ads, carousel ads, or collection ads, to find what resonates best with your audience. Use high-quality visuals, persuasive copywriting, and strong call-to-action buttons to encourage clicks and conversions.

Facebook Advertising for Authors

Setting Budgets and Bidding Strategies:
Facebook Ads Manager allows you to set daily or lifetime budgets for your campaigns. Decide on a budget that aligns with your marketing goals and ensures optimal ad delivery. You can also define your bidding strategy, choosing between automatic bidding or manual bidding to control how you optimize your ad placements and budget allocation.

Ad Placement Options:
Facebook offers various ad placement options to reach your target audience effectively. These include the Facebook News Feed, Instagram Feed, Messenger, Audience Network, and more. Select the ad placements that best align with your audience preferences and campaign objectives.

Monitoring and Optimizing Ad Performance:
Once your ads are live, regularly monitor their performance through Facebook Ads Manager. Analyze metrics such as impressions, click-through rates, conversion rates, and return on ad spend (ROAS). Use this data to identify areas of improvement, refine your targeting, adjust your ad creatives, and optimize your campaigns for better results.

Facebook Ads Manager provides authors with a powerful tool to reach a wider audience and promote their books effectively. By setting clear objectives, defining your target audience, creating compelling ad creatives, and monitoring performance, you can maximize the impact of your Facebook advertising campaigns.

Facebook Advertising for Authors

Creating Your First Ad Campaign

In this section, we will guide you through the process of creating your first ad campaign using Facebook Ads Manager. By following these steps, you can set up a targeted and effective campaign to promote your books and reach your desired audience.

Define Your Advertising Objective:
Begin by selecting the advertising objective that aligns with your goals. Choose from options such as increasing brand awareness, driving traffic to your website, promoting book sales, or generating engagement. Your objective will shape the structure and optimization of your ad campaign.

Choose Your Campaign Type:
Facebook Ads Manager offers various campaign types based on your objective. These include Reach, Traffic, Conversions, and Engagement, among others. Select the campaign type that best aligns with your advertising goals.

Set Up Your Ad Set:
Within your campaign, you'll create an ad set that specifies your target audience, budget, schedule, and placement. Define the demographics, interests, and behaviors of your ideal readers. You can also set a budget for your campaign and determine the duration of your ads.

Facebook Advertising for Authors

Select Ad Placements:
Choose the platforms where you want your ads to appear. Facebook offers a range of placements, including the Facebook News Feed, Instagram, Messenger, and Audience Network. Consider your target audience's preferences and habits to determine the most effective placements for your campaign.

Design Compelling Ad Creatives:
Create captivating ad creatives that will catch the attention of your target audience. Use eye-catching images or videos, persuasive copywriting, and a clear call-to-action. Experiment with different ad formats and variations to see what resonates best with your audience.

Set Ad Budget and Bidding Strategy:
Allocate a budget for your ad set, either on a daily or lifetime basis. Determine how much you're willing to spend on your campaign. Additionally, choose your bidding strategy, whether automatic bidding or manual bidding, to optimize your ad placements and budget allocation.

Ad Tracking and Conversion Measurement:
Set up tracking mechanisms to measure the performance of your ads. Utilize the Facebook pixel to track conversions on your website, such as book purchases or newsletter sign-ups. This data will provide insights into the effectiveness of your campaign and help you make informed decisions for future optimizations.

Monitor and Optimize:
Regularly monitor the performance of your ad campaign through Facebook Ads Manager. Analyze metrics such as reach, impressions, click-through rates, and conversions. Identify areas for improvement and make adjustments to optimize your campaign for better results.

Remember, creating your first ad campaign is an iterative process. Monitor its performance, gather insights, and make data-driven decisions to continually refine and improve your advertising strategy. In the next section, we will explore targeting the right audience to ensure your ads reach the most relevant readers for your books.

Targeting the Right Audience

In this section, we will delve into the importance of targeting the right audience for your Facebook ad campaigns as an author. Facebook offers powerful targeting options that allow you to reach readers who are most likely to be interested in your books. Let's explore how to effectively target the right audience for maximum impact.

Define Your Ideal Reader:
Start by understanding your ideal reader. Consider their demographics, interests, and behaviors. Think about the characteristics of the readers who are most likely to enjoy your genre and writing style. This knowledge forms the foundation for targeting the right audience on Facebook.

Demographic Targeting:

Facebook allows you to target specific demographics, including age, gender, location, and language. Consider the age range and gender that aligns with your target readership. If your books have a specific geographic focus or are available in specific languages, narrow down your targeting accordingly.

Interest-Based Targeting:

Utilize interest-based targeting to reach readers who have shown an interest in topics related to your books. Facebook provides a vast range of interests to choose from. Select interests that align with your genre, themes, and similar authors. This ensures that your ads are delivered to readers who are more likely to engage with your content.

Behavior-Based Targeting:

Take advantage of behavior-based targeting options offered by Facebook. You can target readers based on their behavior patterns, such as purchasing habits, engagement with books or authors, or reading preferences. Refine your targeting to reach readers who exhibit behaviors indicative of your target audience.

Lookalike Audiences:

Consider creating lookalike audiences on Facebook. Lookalike audiences are groups of users who share similar characteristics to your existing audience or customer base. By creating a lookalike audience based on your readers or engaged fans, you can expand your reach to users who are likely to be interested in your books.

Facebook Advertising for Authors

Custom Audiences:
Utilize custom audiences to target specific groups of individuals who are already familiar with your work. You can create custom audiences by uploading your existing mailing list, website visitors, or engaged Facebook fans. Targeting these custom audiences allows you to nurture existing relationships and encourage repeat engagement.

Audience Exclusions:
Refine your audience targeting by excluding certain demographics or interests that may not align with your target readership. This helps ensure that your ads are shown to the most relevant audience and prevents unnecessary ad spend on those unlikely to engage with your books.

Test and Refine:
As you launch your ad campaigns, closely monitor the performance of different audience segments. Evaluate the engagement metrics, conversion rates, and overall campaign success for each audience group.

Targeting the right audience is crucial for the success of your Facebook ad campaigns as an author. By defining your ideal reader, utilizing demographic and interest-based targeting, exploring lookalike and custom audiences, and continuously testing and refining your targeting strategy, you can ensure that your ads reach the readers most likely to be interested in your books.

Budgeting and Bidding Strategies

In this section, we will explore the importance of budgeting and bidding strategies in your Facebook ad campaigns. Effective budget allocation and bidding strategies can optimize your ad delivery, maximize your return on investment, and help you reach your advertising goals as an author.

Determine Your Budget:
Start by determining your overall advertising budget. Consider your marketing goals, the scale of your campaign, and the financial resources available to you. Your budget should align with your objectives and ensure that you have sufficient funds to run your ads effectively over a specific period.

Daily vs. Lifetime Budget:
Facebook Ads Manager offers the option to set either a daily budget or a lifetime budget for your campaigns. A daily budget sets a limit on how much you're willing to spend per day, while a lifetime budget determines your overall spending throughout the duration of your campaign. Choose the budgeting option that suits your campaign goals and financial constraints.

Target Cost and Bid Caps:
Within manual bidding, you can further optimize your bidding strategy by using target cost or bid caps. Target cost allows you to set a target cost per result, such as cost per click (CPC) or cost per thousand impressions (CPM). Bid caps, on the other hand, limit how much you're willing to pay for a specific result. These options help you control your ad spend and optimize your budget allocation.

Ad Auction and Bidding:

Facebook Ads Manager operates on an auction system, where advertisers bid for ad placements. When setting your bidding strategy, you have two options: automatic bidding or manual bidding.

- Automatic Bidding: With automatic bidding, Facebook automatically adjusts your bid to maximize the delivery of your ads while staying within your budget. This option allows Facebook's algorithm to optimize your bids based on your campaign objective.
- Manual Bidding: Manual bidding gives you full control over your bid amount. You set the maximum amount you're willing to bid for each ad placement. This strategy is suitable if you have a specific bid range in mind or if you want more control over your campaign's performance.

Monitor and Adjust:

Regularly monitor the performance of your ad campaigns and adjust your budget and bidding strategies as needed. If you find that your ads are not performing as expected, consider adjusting your bid amounts, targeting, or overall budget to optimize your campaign's performance.

A/B Testing:

Consider conducting A/B tests to determine the most effective bidding strategies for your ad campaigns. Create multiple ad sets with different bidding strategies and compare their performance. This allows you to gather data and insights to refine your bidding approach and allocate your budget more efficiently.

Scale and Iteration:

As you gain more experience and gather data from your ad campaigns, you can scale your budget and bidding strategies accordingly. Gradually increase your budget based on the success and performance of your campaigns. Continuously iterate and optimize your bidding strategies to maximize the return on your advertising investment.

Effective budgeting and bidding strategies are essential for the success of your Facebook ad campaigns. By determining your budget, choosing the appropriate bidding strategy (automatic or manual), utilizing target costs and bid caps, monitoring and adjusting your campaigns, and conducting A/B testing, you can optimize your ad delivery, control your spending, and achieve your advertising goals as an author. In the next section, we will explore different ad formats and creative best practices to make your Facebook ads compelling and engaging.

Ad Formats and Creative Best Practices

By utilizing the right ad formats and implementing creative best practices, you can capture the attention of your target audience and.

Image Ads:
Image ads are a popular and versatile ad format on Facebook. When creating image ads, consider the following best practices:
- Use high-quality, visually appealing images that are relevant to your books and resonate with your target audience.

Facebook Advertising for Authors

- Keep the text overlay minimal and concise, as Facebook has guidelines for the amount of text allowed in image ads.
- Include a clear call-to-action button to encourage users to take the desired action, such as "Learn More" or "Shop Now."

Video Ads:
- Video ads are highly engaging and can capture the attention of your audience effectively. When creating video ads, consider the following best practices:
-
- Keep your videos concise and attention-grabbing, as shorter videos tend to perform better on social media platforms.
- Use compelling visuals, storytelling techniques, and clear messaging to convey the value of your books.
- Incorporate captions or text overlays to ensure your message is understood even without sound, as many users watch videos with the sound off.

Carousel Ads:
- Carousel ads allow you to showcase multiple images or videos within a single ad unit. When using carousel ads, consider the following best practices:
- Tell a story or showcase different aspects of your books by using each carousel card effectively.
- Ensure that each card is visually appealing, with a clear and concise message.
- Experiment with different combinations of images and videos to keep your audience engaged and interested.

Facebook Advertising for Authors

Collection Ads:
- Collection ads are ideal for promoting multiple products or books within a single ad unit. When using collection ads, consider the following best practices:
- Use an attention-grabbing cover image that represents your collection.
- Include compelling product images or book covers within the collection.
- Provide a seamless and immersive experience by linking the ad to a dedicated landing page where users can explore the collection further.

Instant Experience (formerly Canvas):
- Instant Experience ads offer an immersive and interactive experience for users within the Facebook platform. When creating instant experience ads, consider the following best practices:
- Use captivating visuals, engaging storytelling, and interactive elements to provide a unique experience.
- Highlight the key features, benefits, or stories related to your books.
- Include a clear call-to-action button to guide users to the next step, such as exploring more or making a purchase.

Ad Copy Best Practices:
- Regardless of the ad format, compelling ad copy is crucial for driving engagement. Consider the following best practices when writing your ad copy:

- Keep your copy concise and compelling, capturing the essence of your books and intriguing your audience.
- Use clear and persuasive language to convey the value, benefits, or unique selling points of your books.
- Include a strong call-to-action that encourages users to take the desired action, such as "Buy Now," "Download," or "Learn More."

Remember to test different ad formats, visuals, and messaging to identify what resonates best with your audience. Regularly monitor the performance of your ads and make adjustments as needed to optimize your campaigns. In the next chapter, we will explore Facebook tools and integrations that can enhance your author marketing efforts on the platform.

Measuring Success: Understanding Key Metrics

In this final section of Chapter Five, we will explore the key metrics that will help you measure the success of your Facebook ad campaigns. Understanding these metrics is essential for evaluating the performance of your ads, optimizing your strategy, and achieving your advertising goals as an author.

Impressions:
Impressions refer to the number of times your ad was shown on Facebook. It indicates the reach and visibility of your ad campaign. Monitoring impressions can give you an idea of how many people have been exposed to your ads.

Reach:
Reach measures the number of unique individuals who have seen your ads at least once. It provides insights into the actual size of your audience reached by your campaign. Monitoring reach helps you understand the effectiveness of your targeting and ad delivery.

Click-Through Rate (CTR):
CTR calculates the percentage of people who clicked on your ad after seeing it. It is calculated by dividing the number of clicks by the number of impressions. A higher CTR indicates that your ad is engaging and capturing the attention of your audience.

Conversions:
Conversions track the number of desired actions taken by users, such as book purchases, newsletter sign-ups, or downloads. You can set up conversion tracking using the Facebook pixel on your website. Monitoring conversions allows you to measure the effectiveness of your ads in driving tangible results.

Cost per Result:
Cost per result measures the average amount you are spending to achieve a specific outcome, such as a click or conversion. It is calculated by dividing the total amount spent by the number of results obtained. Monitoring cost per result helps you evaluate the efficiency of your ad campaigns and optimize your budget allocation.

Facebook Advertising for Authors

Frequency:
Frequency represents the average number of times a user has seen your ad. It provides insights into how often your ads are being shown to the same individuals. Monitoring frequency helps you manage ad fatigue and ensure your ads are not overly repetitive to your audience.

Engagement Metrics:
Engagement metrics, such as likes, comments, and shares, indicate the level of interaction and interest generated by your ads. Monitoring these metrics helps you gauge the engagement and resonance of your content with your audience.

Audience Insights:
Facebook provides valuable audience insights, such as demographic information, interests, and behaviors of the people engaging with your ads. Analyzing these insights helps you better understand your target audience and refine your targeting strategies.

Regularly monitor and analyze these key metrics to evaluate the performance of your Facebook ad campaigns. Use the insights gained to refine your targeting, adjust your ad creatives, and optimize your budget allocation. By measuring success and making data-driven decisions, you can continually improve the effectiveness of your advertising efforts. In the next chapter, we will explore Facebook tools and integrations that can enhance your author marketing efforts on the platform.

Chapter 5

FACEBOOK TOOLS AND INTEGRATIONS

Using Facebook Pixel to Track Website Conversions

In this chapter, we will explore various Facebook tools and integrations that can enhance your author marketing efforts on the platform. Facebook Pixel is powerful tool for tracking website conversions and optimizing your ad campaigns.

Introduction to Facebook Pixel:
Facebook Pixel is a piece of code provided by Facebook that you can add to your website. It helps you track the actions users take on your website after interacting with your Facebook ads. By installing the Facebook Pixel, you can gain valuable insights into how users engage with your website and measure the effectiveness of your ad campaigns in driving conversions.

Setting Up Facebook Pixel:
To use Facebook Pixel, you need to create a Facebook Business Manager account and set up your Facebook Pixel within the Ads Manager. Follow the step-by-step instructions provided by Facebook to generate the Pixel code. Then, place the code on every page of your website to begin tracking conversions.

Facebook Tools and Integrations

Tracking Website Conversions:
Once Facebook Pixel is installed on your website, it can track various actions taken by users, including purchases, newsletter sign-ups, downloads, or other desired actions. By capturing these conversions, you can assess the success of your ad campaigns and optimize your strategy accordingly.

Custom Conversions:
Facebook Pixel allows you to set up custom conversions, which are specific actions or events you want to track on your website. For example, you can set up a custom conversion to track when a user completes a purchase or signs up for your newsletter. This gives you more granular control over the conversions you want to track and optimize for.

Conversion Optimization:
Facebook Pixel enables conversion optimization, which allows you to target your ads to people who are more likely to take specific actions on your website. By optimizing for conversions, Facebook's algorithm can deliver your ads to users who are more likely to complete the desired actions, such as making a purchase.

Retargeting:
By tracking user behavior on your website, you can create custom audiences of people who have visited specific pages, added items to their cart, or completed certain actions. You can then retarget these audiences with tailored ads to encourage them to take further action.

Facebook Tools and Integrations

Lookalike Audiences:
Facebook Pixel data can also be used to create lookalike audiences. Lookalike audiences are groups of users who share similar characteristics to your existing website visitors or custom audiences. By creating a lookalike audience based on your website visitors, you can expand your reach and target users who are more likely to be interested in your books.

Conversion Tracking and Optimization Tips:
- Ensure that your Facebook Pixel is installed correctly on all relevant pages of your website.
- Regularly monitor the performance of your website conversions through Facebook Ads Manager.
- Use the data provided by Facebook Pixel to optimize your ad campaigns, targeting, and bidding strategies.
- Experiment with different ad creatives, messaging, and landing pages to improve your website conversion rates.
- By using Facebook Pixel to track website conversions, you can gain valuable insights into user behavior, optimize your ad campaigns, and improve your overall marketing strategy as an author. In the next section, we will explore integrating Facebook with your author's website and other social media platforms for a seamless marketing experience.

Integrating Facebook with Your Author Website and Other Social Media

By leveraging these integrations, you can extend your reach, drive traffic to your website, and engage with your audience across multiple channels.

Facebook Tools and Integrations

Adding Social Media Buttons:
Integrate your Facebook presence with your author website by adding social media buttons. Place these buttons prominently on your website, allowing visitors to easily connect with your Facebook Page. This integration encourages users to follow your page.

Embedding Facebook Posts:
Embedding Facebook posts on your author website can increase engagement and encourage users to interact with your content. By embedding posts showcasing book trailers, author interviews, or promotional offers, you can create an interactive experience for visitors, keeping them on your website.

Facebook Like and Share Buttons:
Include Facebook Like and Share buttons on your website's blog posts, book pages, or other relevant content. These buttons allow visitors to easily share your content with their Facebook friends, amplifying your reach and increasing visibility.

Cross-Promoting on Social Media Platforms:
Extend your reach by cross-promoting your Facebook Page and posts on other social media platforms, such as Twitter, Instagram, or LinkedIn. Share excerpts, updates, or links to your Facebook content, encouraging followers on other platforms to connect with you on Facebook. This integration helps drive traffic to your Facebook Page and expands your audience reach.

Facebook Tools and Integrations

Facebook Events Integration:
If you're hosting virtual or physical book launches, signings, or other author events, leverage Facebook Events to create, promote, and manage these events. Integrate your Facebook Events with your author website by embedding event listings or providing direct links to RSVP or ticket purchases.

Facebook Messenger Integration:
Incorporate Facebook Messenger as a communication channel on your website. Add a Messenger chat plugin or a direct link to your Facebook Page's Messenger inbox. This integration enables visitors to reach out to you with questions, inquiries, or feedback directly through Facebook Messenger, fostering direct engagement and building personal connections.

Share Buttons for Website Content:
Integrate social sharing buttons on your website to allow users to share your blog posts, book pages, or other content directly to their Facebook profiles. This integration helps expand your content's reach and drives traffic to your website, increasing your visibility and attracting potential readers.

By integrating Facebook with your author's website and other social media platforms, you create a cohesive and interconnected online presence. It enhances engagement, increases reach, and drives traffic to your website, ultimately supporting your overall author marketing efforts. In the next chapter, we will explore Facebook Insights, a valuable tool for analyzing and understanding data related to your Facebook Page and audience.

Facebook Tools and Integrations

Facebook Insights: Analyzing and Understanding Data

In this final section of Chapter Six, we will explore Facebook Insights, a powerful tool that provides valuable data and analytics about your Facebook Page and audience. By analyzing and understanding this data, you can gain insights into the performance of your content, audience demographics, and engagement metrics, enabling you to make informed decisions to optimize your author marketing strategy.

Accessing Facebook Insights:
Facebook Insights can be accessed through the Insights tab on your Facebook Page. This section provides a comprehensive overview of key metrics related to your Page's performance.

Page Summary:
The Page Summary section in Facebook Insights provides an overview of your Page's performance over a specific period. It includes metrics such as Page likes, post reach, engagement, and actions taken on your Page. This summary gives you a quick snapshot of how your Page is performing and highlights areas that require attention.

Audience Insights:
Audience Insights within Facebook Insights provides detailed information about your Page's audience demographics, interests, and behaviors. It allows you to understand your audience better and tailor your content and targeting strategies accordingly. Explore audience demographics to optimize your content for your target readership.

Facebook Tools and Integrations

Post Performance:
The Post Performance section provides data on the performance of your individual posts. It includes metrics such as reach, engagement (likes, comments, shares), and link clicks. Analyzing this data helps you identify the types of content that resonate most with your audience and adjust your content strategy accordingly.

Timing and Engagement:
Facebook Insights also provides insights into the timing and engagement patterns of your audience. You can view data on when your audience is most active on Facebook, allowing you to schedule your posts for maximum visibility and engagement. Experiment with different posting times to identify the optimal times to reach and engage your audience effectively.

Referral Traffic:
Referral Traffic data shows you which external websites or sources are driving traffic to your Facebook Page. This information helps you understand where your audience is coming from and evaluate the effectiveness of your marketing efforts across various channels. Leverage this data to optimize your promotional activities and focus on the platforms that are generating the most engagement.

Page Views and Actions:
Page Views and Actions data provide insights into how users interact with your Page.

Facebook Tools and Integrations

It includes metrics such as views, average watch time, and engagement. Use this data to assess the performance of your video content, identify trends, and refine your video strategy.

Regularly review and analyze the data provided by Facebook Insights to gain a deeper understanding of your audience, content performance, and overall Page effectiveness. Use these insights to make data-driven decisions, refine your content strategy, and optimize your author marketing efforts on Facebook. In the next chapter, we will explore leveraging Facebook for book launches and promotions, including creating buzz, running promotions, and collaborating with influencers.

Chapter 6

LEVERAGING FACEBOOK FOR BOOK LAUNCHES AND PROMOTIONS

Creating Buzz Before Your Book Launch

In this chapter, we will explore how you can effectively leverage Facebook to generate excitement and create buzz leading up to your book launch. Building anticipation and engaging your audience before the launch can significantly impact the success of your book. Let's delve into strategies for creating buzz on Facebook.

Teaser Campaigns:
Start building anticipation by launching teaser campaigns on Facebook. Share intriguing snippets, quotes, or excerpts from your book to pique the interest of your audience. Create visually appealing graphics or short videos to accompany these teasers. Encourage your followers to share and engage with the teasers to amplify their reach.

Leveraging Facebook for Book Launches and Promotions

Cover Reveal:
Utilize Facebook to unveil the cover of your upcoming book. Create an engaging post with an eye-catching image of the book cover, accompanied by an exciting caption. Consider hosting a live video event for the cover reveal, where you can share insights about the book, its inspiration, or the creative process. Encourage your audience to share the cover reveal post and participate in the conversation.

Exclusive Content:
Reward your Facebook followers by offering them exclusive content related to your book. This could include early access to a chapter, a sneak peek at illustrations, or behind-the-scenes details. Create dedicated Facebook posts or live videos to share this exclusive content, encouraging your audience to engage and share it with others.

Pre-Order Campaign:
Launch a pre-order campaign on Facebook to drive early sales and create a sense of urgency. Share links to online retailers where readers can pre-order your book. Offer incentives for pre-orders, such as signed copies, personalized messages, or limited edition merchandise. Regularly update your Facebook audience on the progress of the pre-order campaign to maintain excitement and encourage more orders.

Leveraging Facebook for Book Launches and Promotions

Interactive Q&A Sessions:

Host interactive Q&A sessions on Facebook Live or through dedicated Facebook posts. Encourage your audience to ask questions about your book, characters, or writing process. This creates a sense of engagement and allows readers to feel involved in the journey leading up to your book launch. Share insights, anecdotes, or behind-the-scenes details to make the sessions engaging and informative.

Influencer Collaborations:

Partner with relevant influencers, book bloggers, or industry professionals on Facebook to amplify your book launch. Collaborate on Facebook posts, live events, or giveaways. Leverage their reach and engage their audience by offering guest posts, interviews, or exclusive content. This collaboration introduces your book to new audiences and enhances its visibility.

Event Listings:

Create Facebook Events for your book launch, signings, or virtual author talks. Customize the event page with captivating visuals, descriptions, and details. Promote the event through Facebook posts, stories, and invitations to build excitement and encourage attendance. Regularly engage with attendees by posting updates, sneak peeks, or reminders leading up to the event.

Leveraging Facebook for Book Launches and Promotions

User-Generated Content:

Encourage your Facebook followers to generate content related to your book. This could include fan art, book reviews, or creative interpretations of your characters. Share and celebrate user-generated content on your Page, tagging and acknowledging the creators. This not only fosters a sense of community but also helps create buzz as others see their peers engaging with your book.

By implementing these strategies, you can effectively create buzz on Facebook and generate excitement leading up to your book launch. Remember to engage with your audience, respond to comments, and thank them for their support. In the next section, we will explore running promotions and contests on Facebook to further engage your audience and drive book sales.

Running Promotions and Contests

In this section, we will explore how you can run promotions and contests on Facebook to engage your audience, generate excitement, and drive book sales. Running promotions and contests can be an effective way to create buzz and encourage interaction with your book launch. Let's delve into strategies for running successful promotions and contests on Facebook.

Giveaway Contests:
Host giveaway contests on Facebook to reward your audience and generate excitement. Encourage users to participate by liking, commenting, sharing, or tagging friends in your contest posts

Leveraging Facebook for Book Launches and Promotions

Ask users to share their favorite book-related stories, experiences, or recommendations to encourage engagement. Offer enticing prizes such as signed copies, book-themed merchandise, or exclusive sneak peeks.

Caption or Quote Contests:
Engage your audience by running caption or quote contests related to your book. Share an image, excerpt, or quote from your book and ask followers to come up with creative captions or share their favorite quotes. Encourage participation by offering book giveaways or featuring winning entries on your social media platforms.

Reader Reviews and Recommendations:
Encourage readers to write reviews or share recommendations for your book on Facebook. Offer incentives such as exclusive content, personalized messages, or shoutouts to participants. Feature selected reviews on your Facebook Page to showcase positive feedback and encourage others to read and review your book.

Fan Art Contests:
Tap into the creativity of your audience by running fan art contests. Encourage readers to create and share their artwork inspired by your book characters or scenes. Establish contest guidelines, such as submission deadlines and artwork requirements. Showcase and celebrate the entries on your Facebook Page, and award prizes to the winners.

Leveraging Facebook for Book Launches and Promotions

Interactive Quizzes and Trivia:
Host interactive quizzes or trivia contests on Facebook to engage your audience and test their knowledge about your book. Share interesting facts, character backgrounds, or plot details, and ask questions related to your book. Offer prizes such as signed copies, book-related merchandise, or exclusive access to future content.

Collaborative Storytelling:
Engage your audience in collaborative storytelling by inviting them to contribute ideas, characters, or plot twists related to your book. Create dedicated Facebook posts or events where users can share their creative input. Acknowledge and incorporate the best suggestions into your storytelling process, giving participants a sense of ownership and involvement.

Virtual Book Club Discussions:
Initiate virtual book club discussions on Facebook to encourage readers to engage with your book and share their thoughts. Create a dedicated Facebook Group or use your Page to facilitate these discussions. Pose questions, provide discussion prompts, and encourage readers to share their interpretations, favorite moments, or book-related discussions.

Promotion Partnerships:
Partner with other authors, publishers, or book-related organizations to run joint promotions on Facebook.

Leveraging Facebook for Book Launches and Promotions

Collaborate on giveaway contests, cross-promote each other's books, or offer exclusive discounts or bundles. Leverage each other's audience reach to expand your visibility and attract new readers.

When running promotions and contests, ensure you comply with Facebook's guidelines and policies. Clearly communicate the rules, eligibility criteria, and deadlines for participation. Regularly engage with participants, respond to comments, and publicly announce winners to maintain transparency and build trust. In the next section, we will explore utilizing Facebook Events for virtual and physical book launches and other author events.

Utilizing Facebook Events for Virtual and Physical Events

In this section, we will explore how you can utilize Facebook Events to effectively promote and manage both virtual and physical events related to your book, such as book launches, signings, author talks, or workshops. Facebook Events provide a convenient platform to reach your audience, generate interest, and encourage attendance. Let's dive into strategies for leveraging Facebook Events.

Creating a Facebook Event:
To create a Facebook Event, navigate to your Facebook Page and click on the "Create Event" button. Fill in the event details, including the event name, date, time, location (if applicable), description, and event image.

Leveraging Facebook for Book Launches and Promotions

Customize the event page with eye-catching visuals, intriguing descriptions, and relevant event information.

Virtual Events:
For virtual events, such as online book launches or author talks, select the "Online Event" option when creating the Facebook Event. Provide details on how users can join the virtual event, whether it's through a livestream on your Facebook Page, a webinar platform, or a dedicated website. Include clear instructions on how attendees can participate and engage during the event.

Physical Events:
For physical events, such as book signings or author appearances, select the appropriate location when creating the Facebook Event. Include the venue details, address, and any additional information attendees need to know, such as entry fees, registration requirements, or special instructions. Consider creating a visually appealing event cover photo to attract attention.

Event Descriptions:
Craft compelling and informative event descriptions that highlight the unique aspects and benefits of attending your event. Share details about what attendees can expect, such as book readings, author Q&A sessions, or exclusive giveaways. Use engaging language to create excitement and encourage people to RSVP and share the event with their friends.

Leveraging Facebook for Book Launches and Promotions

Event Updates and Reminders:
Regularly post updates, sneak peeks, or reminders on the Facebook Event page to maintain momentum and keep attendees engaged. Share behind-the-scenes insights, exclusive content, or teasers to build anticipation. Consider creating a countdown series leading up to the event to generate excitement and encourage attendance.

Attendee Engagement:
Encourage attendee engagement by creating interactive posts, asking questions, or hosting polls on the Facebook Event page. Respond promptly to attendee comments and questions to foster a sense of community and build excitement. Encourage attendees to invite their friends, share the event, and tag people who might be interested.

Post-Event Follow-Up:
After the event, show appreciation to attendees by posting thank-you messages or event recaps on the Facebook Event page. Share highlights, photos, or videos from the event to keep the momentum going. Encourage attendees to share their experiences and feedback, and consider running post-event contests or giveaways to maintain engagement.

By utilizing Facebook Events effectively, you can effectively promote and manage your virtual and physical events, ensuring maximum attendance and engagement.

Leveraging Facebook for Book Launches and Promotions

Leverage the features and engagement opportunities provided by Facebook Events to build anticipation, generate buzz, and create memorable experiences for your audience. In the next chapter, we will explore setting up a Facebook Shop and leveraging e-commerce for selling books and merchandise directly through Facebook.

Collaborating with Book Bloggers and Influencers

In this section, we will explore the benefits of collaborating with book bloggers and influencers on Facebook to amplify your book's reach and engagement. These collaborations can help you tap into established audiences, generate buzz, and increase your book's visibility. Let's delve into strategies for collaborating with book bloggers and influencers on Facebook.

Identifying Book Bloggers and Influencers:
Research and identify book bloggers and influencers on Facebook who align with your book's genre, target audience, and interests. Look for bloggers with an engaged following and a demonstrated interest in promoting books. Explore their Facebook Pages or profiles to assess their content quality, engagement levels, and audience demographics.

Personalized Outreach:
Reach out to book bloggers and influencers individually with personalized messages expressing your interest in collaborating.

Leveraging Facebook for Book Launches and Promotions

Highlight why you believe your book would resonate with their audience and how the collaboration could be mutually beneficial. Be specific about the type of collaboration you have in mind, such as book reviews, author interviews, or guest posts.

Guest Blogging or Takeovers:
Collaborate with book bloggers and influencers by offering to write guest blog posts or taking over their Facebook Page for a specified period. Craft engaging and informative posts related to your book, writing process, or book-related topics. Provide exclusive content, insights, or behind-the-scenes stories to captivate their audience and encourage engagement.

Book Reviews and Recommendations:
Request book reviews or recommendations from book bloggers and influencers. Offer them a complimentary copy of your book and ask for an honest review or recommendation on their Facebook Page. Ensure they disclose any sponsored content or gifted copies as per ethical guidelines. Positive reviews from respected influencers can significantly impact book sales and generate buzz.

Influencer Takeovers:
Organize influencer takeovers on your Facebook Page, where a book blogger or influencer temporarily assumes control to engage with your audience. This can include live videos, Q&A sessions, or curated content. Promote the takeover event in your Facebook Page to attract their audience and encourage participation.

Leveraging Facebook for Book Launches and Promotions

Giveaways and Collaborative Contests:
Collaborate with book bloggers and influencers to host joint giveaways or contests on Facebook. Pool resources to offer enticing prizes, such as book bundles, exclusive merchandise, or personalized book experiences. Co-promote the contest on both your Facebook Pages to reach a wider audience and encourage engagement.

Affiliate Partnerships:
Consider affiliate partnerships with book bloggers or influencers who have a strong presence on Facebook. Provide them with personalized affiliate links or discount codes to share with their audience. In return, they earn a commission or other incentives for every book sale generated through their unique links. This mutually beneficial partnership encourages influencers to actively promote your book.

Sponsored Content:
Explore opportunities for sponsored content with book bloggers and influencers. Negotiate sponsored posts, shoutouts, or sponsored live videos on their Facebook Pages. Ensure that sponsored content aligns with their usual content style and maintains authenticity. Collaborate on creating engaging content that highlights your book's unique selling points and resonates with their audience.

Chapter 7

FACEBOOK SHOPS AND E-COMMERCE FOR AUTHORS

Setting Up Facebook Shop

In this chapter, we will explore how authors can leverage Facebook Shops and e-commerce to sell their books and merchandise directly on Facebook. Setting up a Facebook Shop provides a convenient and seamless shopping experience for your audience, allowing them to browse and purchase your products without leaving the platform. Let's delve into the steps for setting up your Facebook Shop.

Eligibility and Requirements:
Before setting up a Facebook Shop, ensure that you meet the eligibility requirements. Typically, you need to have a Facebook Page for your author brand and comply with Facebook's merchant policies. Check Facebook's guidelines to confirm your eligibility and familiarize yourself with any specific requirements for selling books and merchandise.

Facebook Shops and E-commerce for Authors

Accessing Commerce Manager:
To set up your Shop, access the Commerce Manager on your Facebook Page. Navigate to your Page, click on the "Settings" tab, and select "Commerce Manager" from the left-hand menu. Follow the prompts to get started with setting up your shop.

Shop Setup:
Within the Commerce Manager, select the "Set Up Shop" option. You will be guided through a series of steps to configure your shop. Provide essential details such as your business information, product categories, and shipping options. Ensure that your product descriptions are clear, informative, and include relevant keywords to improve discoverability.

Product Listings:
Once your shop is set up, it's time to add product listings. Include your books, merchandise, and any other items you want to sell. Provide high-quality product images, accurate descriptions, and pricing details. If you have multiple variations (e.g., different book formats or merchandise sizes), specify them clearly within the listings.

Shop Design and Customization:
Customize the appearance of your Facebook Shop to align with your brand. Choose a visually appealing cover image and ensure your shop layout is intuitive and user-friendly. Leverage Facebook's customization options to create a cohesive and attractive shopping experience for your audience.

Facebook Shops and E-commerce for Authors

Integration with E-commerce Platform:
To process payments and manage orders, integrate your Facebook Shop with an e-commerce platform or payment provider. Facebook supports integration with various platforms, such as Shopify, WooCommerce, or BigCommerce. Follow the instructions provided by your chosen platform to connect it with your Facebook Shop.

Shop Management:
Regularly monitor your Facebook Shop to manage product inventory, process orders, and respond to customer inquiries. Use the Commerce Manager to track sales, fulfill orders, and handle customer support. Set up notifications and alerts to ensure prompt responses to customer messages and order updates.

Promoting Your Facebook Shop:
Once your Facebook Shop is set up, promote it to your audience across various channels. Share posts, stories, and ads on Facebook, directing followers to your shop. Leverage other social media platforms, your author website, newsletter, and blog to drive traffic to your Facebook Shop. Consider running targeted ads to reach potential readers who may be interested in your books.

By setting up a Facebook Shop, you can provide a seamless shopping experience for your audience, making it easier for them to purchase your books and merchandise directly on Facebook.

Facebook Shops and E-commerce for Authors

Regularly update your product listings, monitor inventory, and provide excellent customer service to maintain a positive shopping experience. In the next section, we will explore strategies for handling negative feedback, managing online reputation, and maintaining professionalism on Facebook.

Selling Books and Merchandise Directly Through Facebook

In this section, we will explore strategies for effectively selling your books and merchandise directly through your Facebook Shop. By leveraging the features and tools available within Facebook Shops, you can optimize your product listings, engage your audience, and drive sales.

Compelling Product Descriptions:
Craft compelling and informative product descriptions for your books and merchandise. Highlight key features, benefits, and unique selling points to entice potential buyers. Use clear and concise language, and include relevant keywords to improve discoverability within Facebook's search function.

High-Quality Product Images:
Ensure your product images are high-quality and visually appealing. Use professional-quality photographs or well-designed graphics to showcase your books and merchandise. Show different angles, close-ups, or product details to give buyers a comprehensive view.

Facebook Shops and E-commerce for Authors

Pricing and Special Offers:
Price your books and merchandise competitively based on market research and your target audience's expectations. Consider offering special promotions, discounts, or bundles to incentivize purchases. Use Facebook's promotional tools to drive urgency and encourage conversions.

Call-to-Action Buttons:
Optimize your Facebook Shop by utilizing call-to-action buttons effectively. Place prominent "Shop Now" or "Buy" buttons on your product listings to encourage direct purchases. Customize the button text to create a sense of urgency or highlight any special offers, such as "Limited Stock" or "Exclusive Edition."

Cross-Promotion:
Leverage the cross-promotion capabilities within Facebook Shops to showcase related products or recommend complementary items. For example, if someone is viewing one of your books, display other books in the series or similar genres. Encourage customers to explore more of your offerings, increasing the likelihood of multiple purchases.

Customer Reviews and Ratings:
Encourage customers who have purchased your books or merchandise to leave reviews and ratings on Facebook. Positive reviews can build trust and influence potential buyers. Monitor and respond to customer reviews promptly, addressing any concerns or issues raised. This demonstrates your commitment to customer satisfaction and enhances your reputation.

Facebook Shops and E-commerce for Authors

Customer Support:
Provide excellent customer support to enhance the shopping experience. Respond to customer inquiries, messages, or comments in a timely and professional manner. Address any issues or concerns promptly and resolve them to the best of your ability. Prompt and attentive customer support can foster customer loyalty and encourage repeat purchases.

Promote and Share:
Regularly promote your Facebook Shop and product listings to your audience. Share posts, stories, or ads highlighting specific books, merchandise, or limited-time offers. Leverage Facebook's targeting options to reach specific demographics or interest groups who are likely to be interested in your products. Encourage your audience to share your posts and spread the word about your books and merchandise.

By implementing these strategies, you can effectively sell your books and merchandise directly through your Facebook Shop. Continuously monitor your shop's performance, track sales metrics, and make adjustments as needed to optimize your sales efforts. In the next chapter, we will explore strategies for handling negative feedback, managing your online reputation, and maintaining professionalism on Facebook.

Chapter 8

CRISIS MANAGEMENT AND ONLINE ETIQUETTE

Handling Negative Feedback and Criticism

In this chapter, we will discuss strategies for effectively managing negative feedback and criticism on Facebook. As an author with an online presence, it's essential to handle such situations with professionalism and empathy. By addressing negative feedback constructively, you can maintain your reputation, build trust with your audience, and turn negative experiences into positive ones. Let's delve into strategies for handling negative feedback and criticism on Facebook.

Monitor and Respond Promptly:
Regularly monitor your Facebook Page for any negative comments, reviews, or messages. Respond to negative feedback promptly, acknowledging the concerns raised. Even if you can't provide an immediate solution, a timely response shows that you care about your readers and are actively addressing their concerns.

Crisis Management and Online Etiquette

Remain Calm and Professional:
When responding to negative feedback, maintain a calm and professional tone. Avoid responding defensively or engaging in heated arguments. Take the time to understand the issue and respond thoughtfully. Remember to maintaining professionalism.

Empathize and Acknowledge Concerns:
Show empathy towards the individual expressing negative feedback. Acknowledge their concerns and validate their feelings. Let them know that you understand their frustration and that their feedback is valuable to you.

Seek Feedback from Trusted Sources:
It's also beneficial to seek feedback from trusted sources such as colleagues, mentors, or industry professionals. Share your work with them and ask for their honest opinions and constructive criticism. Their perspectives can provide valuable insights and help you identify areas for improvement.

Use Feedback as a Learning Opportunity:
Negative feedback and criticism can be challenging to receive, but it's important to view them as opportunities for learning and growth. Rather than taking feedback personally, approach it with an open mind and a willingness to improve. Reflect on the feedback received and consider how it aligns with your goals and values as an author. Use it as a chance to reassess your writing style, content strategy, or communication approach. By embracing feedback as a valuable tool, you can continuously evolve and deliver a better experience for your readers.

Crisis Management and Online Etiquette

Demonstrating empathy can help defuse tension and foster a more constructive conversation.

Take the Conversation Offline:
If the negative feedback requires a detailed discussion or resolution, encourage the individual to continue the conversation privately through direct messages or email. This allows for a more personalized and focused exchange, where you can address their concerns more thoroughly and find a suitable solution.

Offer Solutions or Compensations:
When appropriate, offer solutions or compensations to address the concerns raised. Depending on the situation, this could include providing additional information, replacing a faulty product, or offering a refund. Tailor your response to the specific issue and strive to find a resolution that satisfies the customer.

Respond Publicly, Resolve Privately:
While it's important to acknowledge negative feedback publicly, it's equally crucial to respect the privacy of individuals. Avoid discussing personal or sensitive information publicly. Once the issue has been resolved privately, circle back to the original comment or post to provide a brief update, showcasing your commitment to resolving concerns.

Encourage Constructive Dialogue:
In situations where negative feedback sparks a broader discussion, encourage dialogue among your audience.

Crisis Management and Online Etiquette

Ensure that the conversation remains respectful and focused on addressing the issue at hand. Moderate the discussion, intervene when necessary, and provide clarifications or additional information to guide the conversation.

Learn and Improve:
View negative feedback as an opportunity for growth and improvement. Analyze recurring concerns or patterns in feedback and consider them as constructive feedback for your future work. By actively listening and making improvements based on feedback, you can enhance your writing, communication, and overall reader experience.

By implementing these strategies, you can effectively handle negative feedback and criticism on Facebook. Remember, addressing negative feedback with empathy, professionalism, and a commitment to finding solutions can help you maintain a positive online reputation and build stronger connections with your audience. In the next section, we will explore strategies for managing your online reputation and maintaining professionalism in the digital age.

Managing Your Online Reputation

In this section, we will explore strategies for effectively managing your online reputation on Facebook as an author. Your online reputation plays a crucial role in how readers perceive you and your work. By proactively managing your online presence and reputation, you can maintain a positive image and build trust with your audience.

Crisis Management and Online Etiquette

Consistent Branding:

Maintain consistent branding across your Facebook Page and other online platforms. Use a professional and high-quality profile and cover photos that reflect your author brand. Ensure your bio or about section clearly communicates your identity as an author and the genre or themes of your work. Consistency in branding helps establish recognition and credibility.

Thoughtful Content Curation:

Be mindful of the content you share on your Facebook Page. Curate content that aligns with your brand values, resonates with your audience, and adds value to their lives. Share relevant industry news, writing tips, book recommendations, or insights into your creative process. Thoughtful content curation reinforces your expertise and fosters engagement.

Engage Authentically:

Engage authentically with your audience on Facebook. Respond to comments, messages, and mentions in a timely manner. Show appreciation for positive feedback, answer questions, and actively participate in discussions related to your books or writing. Authentic engagement demonstrates your accessibility and builds a positive rapport with your readers.

Encourage and Showcase Positive Reviews:

Encourage readers to leave positive reviews and ratings on your Facebook Page. Share these reviews or testimonials on your Page, highlighting the positive experiences of your readers.

Crisis Management and Online Etiquette

This helps build social proof and enhances your credibility as an author. Regularly monitor and respond to reviews, expressing gratitude for the support.

Monitor Mentions and Tags:
Stay vigilant and monitor mentions and tags related to your author brand on Facebook. Set up notifications for these mentions so that you can respond promptly. Engage with users who tag you in posts or comments, acknowledging their interaction and showing appreciation. Monitoring mentions allows you to stay aware of your online presence and address any concerns or issues raised.

Address Misinformation or Misrepresentation:
If you come across misinformation or misrepresentation of your work, take appropriate steps to address it. Respond respectfully, providing accurate information or clarifications. Consider addressing the issue publicly, demonstrating your commitment to transparency and accuracy. Be proactive in setting the record straight to maintain the integrity of your author brand.

Foster Positive Relationships with Influencers:
Cultivate positive relationships with influencers and book bloggers in the industry. Collaborate with them on joint projects, guest posts, or promotions. Engaging with influencers who align with your values can help amplify your positive reputation and broaden your reach. Nurture these relationships through ongoing interactions and support.

Crisis Management and Online Etiquette

Monitor Online Discussions and Reviews:
Regularly monitor online discussions and reviews related to your books or author brand. Be aware of what readers are saying about your work and actively participate in relevant conversations. Respond respectfully to both positive and negative feedback, showcasing your willingness to engage and address concerns.

By implementing these strategies, you can effectively manage your online reputation on Facebook. Consistent branding, thoughtful content curation, authentic engagement, and proactive monitoring are key to building a positive reputation as an author. Remember, maintaining professionalism and fostering positive relationships are integral to managing your online presence. In the next chapter, we will explore the evolving nature of Facebook and social media, and strategies for staying updated on industry trends and best practices.

Staying Professional in the Digital Age

In this section, we will discuss strategies for maintaining professionalism on Facebook as an author in the digital age. As social media continues to evolve, it's essential to uphold a professional image that aligns with your author brand. By implementing certain practices and guidelines, you can navigate the digital landscape with professionalism and integrity. Let's delve into strategies for staying professional in the digital age.

Crisis Management and Online Etiquette

Be Mindful of Your Language and Tone:
Choose your words carefully and be mindful of your tone when engaging on Facebook. Use language that reflects professionalism and respect. Avoid using offensive or derogatory language, and refrain from engaging in online arguments or personal attacks. Maintain a polite and constructive approach in all interactions.

Separate Personal and Professional Accounts:
Consider creating separate personal and professional accounts on Facebook. This allows you to maintain a clear distinction between your personal life and your author brand. Keep your professional account focused on author-related content, book promotions, and interactions with readers, while reserving personal matters for your personal account.

Set Boundaries:
Establish clear boundaries for your online presence. Decide how much personal information you are comfortable sharing and stick to those boundaries. Avoid oversharing personal details that are unrelated to your author's brand. By maintaining a professional distance, you can protect your privacy and maintain a clear focus on your writing career.

Fact-Check Before Sharing:
Before sharing content on your Facebook Page, take the time to fact-check and verify its accuracy. Ensure that the information you share is reliable, credible, and from reputable sources.

Crisis Management and Online Etiquette

Avoid sharing misleading or false information that could damage your professional reputation. By being diligent in your content sharing, you uphold your credibility as an author.

Practice Netiquette:
Adhere to netiquette guidelines when engaging on Facebook. Be respectful of others' opinions, even if you disagree with them. Avoid offensive or inflammatory comments. Use proper grammar, spelling, and punctuation in your posts and comments. Display professionalism in all your online interactions.

Maintain a Consistent Schedule:
Be consistent in your Facebook activities and postings. Develop a schedule that aligns with your goals and the audience's expectations. Regularly update your Facebook Page with valuable content, promotions, or updates. Consistency demonstrates your commitment to your readers and helps build a reliable and professional image.

Be Transparent and Authentic:
Maintain transparency and authenticity in your interactions on Facebook. Be genuine and honest in your communications. Acknowledge any mistakes or errors gracefully and take responsibility when necessary. By being transparent and authentic, you build trust with your audience and maintain a professional reputation.

Continuous Learning and Adaptation:
Stay updated on Facebook's policies, features, and best practices. Regularly seek out professional development resources and industry trends to enhance your knowledge. Adapt to the changing digital landscape by embracing new technologies and strategies. By continuously learning and evolving, you position yourself as a professional author in the digital age.

By implementing these strategies, you can navigate the digital landscape on Facebook with professionalism and integrity. Upholding a professional image, setting boundaries, practicing netiquette, and staying informed are key to maintaining a positive online presence. Remember, your professionalism on Facebook can significantly impact your author brand and audience perception. In the conclusion, we will recap the key points covered in this book and provide additional resources for continued learning.

Chapter 9

STAYING UPDATED AND ADAPTING TO CHANGES

The Evolving Nature of Facebook and Social Media

In today's fast-paced digital world, staying updated on the evolving nature of Facebook and social media is of paramount importance for authors. With the continuous advancements and changes in technology, it is crucial for authors to adapt their strategies and stay abreast of the latest features, trends, and best practices. By doing so, authors can effectively leverage the power of social media platforms like Facebook to connect with their audience, build a strong online presence, and promote their work.

Facebook, being one of the leading social media platforms, undergoes frequent updates and introduces new features to enhance user experience. As an author, keeping up with these changes can offer valuable opportunities to expand your reach and engage with your readers. By staying updated, you can take advantage of new features such as Facebook Live, Stories, or Groups, which provide interactive and immersive ways to connect with your audience.

Staying Updated and Adapting to Changes

Rapid Changes in Social Media:
Social media platforms, including Facebook, are continuously evolving to meet the changing needs and preferences of users. New features, algorithms, and policies are introduced regularly. It's important to stay informed about these updates to maximize your reach and engagement on Facebook.

Keep Up with Platform Changes:
Follow official Facebook announcements, newsletters, and blog updates to stay informed about platform changes. Facebook often releases new features and updates its algorithms to enhance user experiences. By keeping up with these changes, you can adjust your social media marketing strategies accordingly.

Industry News and Resources:
Stay connected to industry news and resources focused on social media marketing. Subscribe to reputable blogs, newsletters, and podcasts that provide insights into the latest trends and best practices. Engage with online communities, forums, and social media groups where professionals share knowledge and discuss industry updates.

Continuous Learning:
Invest time in continuous learning to enhance your social media marketing skills. Attend webinars, workshops, and conferences related to social media marketing and Facebook strategies. Engage in online courses or certifications that provide in-depth knowledge on leveraging social media platforms effectively.

Staying Updated and Adapting to Changes

Experiment and Adapt:
Embrace a mindset of experimentation and adaptation. Social media platforms evolve rapidly, and what works today may not work tomorrow. Be willing to try new strategies, test different content formats, and analyze the results. Adapt your approach based on audience feedback and changing algorithms to stay ahead of the curve.

User Behavior and Trends:
Monitor user behavior and social media trends to align your Facebook marketing efforts with the preferences of your target audience. Stay updated on how users engage with content, the rise of new formats (such as video or live streaming), and emerging trends in your specific genre or industry.

Embrace New Formats and Features:
Be open to embracing new formats and features introduced by Facebook. For example, consider leveraging Facebook Live for author Q&A sessions or virtual book readings. Explore the potential of Facebook Stories to share behind-the-scenes content or exclusive sneak peeks. Embracing new features allows you to engage your audience in unique and compelling ways.

Analyze and Optimize:
Regularly analyze the performance of your Facebook marketing efforts using Facebook Insights, third-party analytics tools, or performance metrics provided by e-commerce platforms. Identify patterns, trends, and areas for improvement.

Staying Updated and Adapting to Changes

By staying updated on the evolving nature of Facebook and social media, you can adapt your marketing strategies to leverage new features, engage your audience effectively, and stay ahead of the competition. Continuous learning, monitoring industry trends, and embracing experimentation are key to thriving in the dynamic digital landscape. In the conclusion, we will recap the key points covered in this book and provide additional resources for your continued learning journey.

Staying Informed on Industry Trends and Best Practices

In this section, we will explore strategies for staying informed about industry trends and best practices in social media marketing, specifically focusing on Facebook. Staying up-to-date on industry trends ensures that your marketing strategies remain effective and relevant. Let's delve into strategies for staying informed on industry trends and best practices.

Follow Industry Leaders and Influencers:
Identify key industry leaders and influencers in social media marketing, particularly those who specialize in Facebook marketing. Follow their blogs, social media accounts, and newsletters to gain insights into the latest trends, strategies, and case studies. Engage with their content and learn from their experiences.

Join Professional Associations and Groups:
Become a member of professional associations or groups that focus on social media marketing or digital marketing as a whole.

Staying Updated and Adapting to Changes

These associations often provide valuable resources, webinars, and networking opportunities to keep you informed about industry trends and best practices. Engage in discussions and share knowledge with fellow professionals.

Attend Conferences and Webinars:
Participate in social media marketing conferences, webinars, and workshops. These events offer opportunities to learn from industry experts, gain insights into emerging trends, and connect with like-minded professionals. Stay updated on the latest events in the field and prioritize attending those that align with your specific interests and goals.

Engage in Online Communities:
Join online communities, forums, and social media groups where professionals discuss social media marketing. Participate in discussions, ask questions, and share your experiences. These communities are excellent sources of knowledge, and you can gain valuable insights into current trends, challenges, and best practices.

Follow Facebook's Official Resources:
Stay connected with Facebook's official resources, including their official blog, business pages, and updates. Facebook often shares insights, tips, and best practices to help marketers make the most of the platform. Stay updated on any policy changes, algorithm updates, or new features that Facebook announces.

Staying Updated and Adapting to Changes

Monitor Social Media News and Publications:
Keep an eye on social media news and publications that cover the latest trends, research studies, and case studies in social media marketing. Websites and publications like Social Media Examiner, Hootsuite Blog, and Buffer Blog regularly publish valuable content to help marketers stay informed and up-to-date.

Analyze Competitor Strategies:
Monitor the social media strategies of your competitors, especially authors in your genre. Analyze their Facebook presence, content strategies, engagement tactics, and promotional activities. While you should never copy their strategies, observing competitor tactics can inspire new ideas and help you understand industry trends.

Continuous Learning:
Commit to continuous learning in social media marketing. Read books, listen to podcasts, and take online courses that focus on Facebook marketing and social media strategies. Stay curious and embrace a growth mindset that encourages you to continually improve your knowledge and skills.

By staying informed on industry trends and best practices, you can refine your Facebook marketing strategies and stay ahead of the curve. The ever-changing nature of social media demands a proactive approach to learning and adapting. Regularly explore new resources, engage with industry experts, and stay open to experimenting with emerging trends.

www.ingramcontent.com/pod-product-compliance
Lightning Source LLC
Chambersburg PA
CBHW050317230526
45471CB00005B/2220